LEGENDS
OF THE MISSISSAUGAS

LEGENDS
OF THE MISSISSAUGAS

by W. Gordon Mills

With Illustrations by
Saul Mamakeesick

Published by

Distributed by
Natural Heritage/Natural History Inc.

Copyright © J. Murray Speirs and John W. Sabean, 1992

All rights reserved. No part of this publication may be reproduced in any manner whatsoever without permission in writing from the publisher, except by a reviewer who wishes to quote brief passages for inclusion in a review.

Canadian Cataloguing in Publication Data

Mills, W. Gordon, 1886–1960

Legends of the Mississaugas

Poem

Includes bibliographical references

ISBN 0-9695729-0-5

1. Mississauga Indians—Legends—Poetry

I. Mamakeesick, Saul, 1957–   II. Title

PS8526.155L4 1992   C811'.52   C92-093201-0

PR9199.2.M55L4 1992

Doris Huestis Speirs

is the inspiration behind the publication

of *Legends of the Mississaugas*. Mrs. Speirs was the wife of Gordon Mills in 1923

when the poem was written. The poem remained in her possession. She planned

its publication, commissioned the art work, and prepared the manuscript. Unfortunately, she

died before the poem found a publisher.

The publisher is indebted to a number of people for their generous assistance in seeing

this book through publication. First and foremost is Dr. J. Murray Speirs, husband of the late

Doris Huestis Speirs, who was the driving force behind the final stages of publication.

Craig Barrett, Carol Sabean, Kim Fox, and Sheila Maki also freely gave their

advice and assistance.

Design: John Cormier **Production:** Helen Piilonen

Photography: See Spot Run **Colour Separations:** Image Dynamics Corp.

Printed and bound in Canada by Spinnaker Graphics Inc.

◆◆◆

INTRODUCTION
The Mississaugas

The Mississaugas were a band of the Ojibwas, one of the four tribal groups of the Algonquian linguistic family. In their own language the members of this family called themselves Anishinabe (plural, Anishinabeg). The Anishinabeg were originally settled in the lands to the north of Lakes Superior and Huron. However, late in the seventeenth century they began to take advantage of the weakened condition of the Iroquois to migrate southward. They drove the Iroquois out of present-day southern Ontario and settled themselves along the north shore of Lakes Ontario and Erie. The warfare between the two great Native nations had been fierce and enmity lingered long after the event. The Anishinabeg called the Iroquois Natowè, their word for snake.

Most of the Mississauga band settled in the area of the lower Credit River. The British purchased the land from them in 1805 and 1818. The Mississauga resettled on a reserve north of the mouth of the Credit in 1826, but moved to the Grand River Reserve, near Brantford, Ontario, in 1847. A few scattered bands also settled in such places as Scugog Island, Rice Lake, and Chemong Lake.

The Anishinabeg, like other Native groups in North America, have a great body of mythological and legendary tales. These tales were repeated to preserve the history and traditions of the tribe, to instruct the young, and to entertain. The stories were told on long winter evenings as the people gathered around the campfires. Many tribes even forbade the telling of tales in the summer (see p. 26):

Never tell a tale in summer
Lest the animals should hear you:
Lest they hear and be offended:
....
Winter is the time for stories....

Among the stories that were told were myths of creation that describe the origin of the world and the interrelatedness of its elements. The stories were of three basic types: Earth Diver myths, where the Great Spirit dives or orders various animals to dive into primeval waters to bring up mud, out of which he fashions the Earth; Trickster myths, where a trickster/magician steals fire, or light, or some other element and either loses them or sets them loose to create the world; Cultural Hero myths, where a human being of supernatural powers creates the world. A prominent figure in these myths is Nanabozho (or Nanabush), who plays a dual role as both the hero/creator and the trickster/magician. The stories vary greatly with the telling. In the version presented here, Nanabozho is the great creator and benefactor of humankind.

The source for W. Gordon Mills' knowledge of the Mississaugas was undoubtedly Alexander Francis Chamberlain's studies. Chamberlain visited the Mississaugas of Scugog Island in 1888 and three years later completed a PhD thesis for the anthropology department at Clark University. He presented the first printed copy of his thesis to the Toronto Public Library in 1892, "in grateful remembrance of its utility and services to the Public at large and to students of Science …." This thesis, as well as a number of Chamberlain's articles in the *Journal of American Folk-lore* would have been readily available to Mills. Chamberlain had expressed a concern that the tales and legends would soon be forgotten. In 1888, he wrote: "These stories are only known to the older generation … and will soon be lost to oblivion if not taken down at once."

There are also several other possible sources for Mills' research. He may have known of Peter Jones' *History of the Ojebway Indians*, in which Jones, a member of the Mississauga band and a Methodist minister, briefly summarizes the creation legend (London: A.W. Bennett, 1861, pp. 32-36). Henry Schoolcraft, an American ethnologist, had published a collection of Ojibway tales in 1839 *(Algic Researches)* on which Henry Wadsworth Longfellow had based his *Song of Hiawatha*. Donald Smith's *Sacred Feathers: The Reverend Peter Jones (Kahkewaquonaby) and the Mississauga Indians* (Toronto: University of Toronto Press, 1987) provides the best recent review of the literature on the Mississaugas.

Wilfrid Gordon Mills

Legends of the Mississaugas was written in 1923. The author, Wilfrid Gordon Mills, a 37-year-old executive with the T. Eaton Company in Toronto, was a man of many talents. He was a statesman, an art patron, an organist and church leader, and an occasional poet. Born in Brantford, Ontario, in 1886, Mills moved with his family to Toronto where he was schooled at Rose Avenue Public School and Jarvis Street Collegiate. He first joined the T. Eaton Company in 1918, remaining with the company until 1935, when he suffered a nervous breakdown. He was Assistant Manager of the Treasury Department in charge of investments, 1918–1922; Head of Advertising and Public Relations, 1922–1929; and Personnel Staff Superintendent, 1929–1935.

Gordon Mills' first work in public service came during the First World War when he was asked to organize the Toronto and York Patriotic Fund. Later he joined the aviation branch of the Imperial Munitions Board. In the Second World War, Mills was appointed director of the inspection division for the armed forces. He quickly moved up to Assistant Deputy Minister of National Defence for Naval Services and then to Deputy Minister with a seat on the Naval Board as the financial and civil member. In 1943, he was named a Companion of the Order of Saint Michael and Saint George (CMG), in recognition of his wartime service.

Born into a Methodist family, Gordon Mills served as organist and choir master of the Carlton Street Methodist Church. Later, he and his parents left the Methodist church for the Christian Science church. In the 1920s, he was an organist at the First Church of Christ, Scientist, Toronto. He was also on the advisory council of the Toronto Conservatory of Music. In the late 1930s, he gave private lessons in New York and Boston during his time of recovery from his nervous breakdown. Mills also served as First Reader of the Toronto Christian Science church from 1924 to 1927, and as First Reader of Ottawa's First Church from 1955 to 1958, when he retired and moved to Thornhill.

Mills was a member of the council for the Art Gallery of Toronto in the 1920s. Among his close friends were Lawren Harris, J.E.H. MacDonald, and other members of the Group of Seven. Gordon Mills and his wife Doris first became acquainted with people in the art world through their membership in the Christian Science church. Fred and Bess Housser, fellow Christian Scientists, were their best friends in those years. Fred Housser was later to write the first history of the Group of Seven: *A Canadian Art Movement: the Story of the Group of Seven* (Toronto: Macmillan, 1926). J.E.H. MacDonald's wife Joan, Lawren Harris' mother Anna Raynolds, and Franz Johnston were also members of the Christian Science church.

In 1923, Mills wrote 35 poems, most of which were written during holidays at Scarborough Beach, Maine. Of these, by far the longest is *Legends of the Mississaugas*. Mills' usual subjects for his poems were music, nature, and art, most of which were also interests of his friend Lawren Harris who was also the first major influence on Mills as a poet. After some long discussions with Harris in the summer and early fall of 1921, Mills wrote his first poem on 10 October 1921, and he continued to write poems for the rest of his life. Harris, himself, published a book of poems in 1922: *Contrasts: A Book of Verse* (Toronto: McClelland & Stewart). A number of Mills' poems were published during his lifetime by the *Christian Science Monitor*. A selection of his poems were published in 1985: *Timber Line and Other Poems*, ed. Doris Huestis Speirs (Toronto: Natural Heritage/ Natural History).

Saul Mamakeesick

Saul Mamakeesick was born in 1957 on the Sandy Lake Indian Reserve in northwestern Ontario. He is of mixed Cree and Ojibway ancestry. Sandy Lake was also the birthplace of the Woodland School, one of the major centres of contemporary Native art. Although Saul is largely self-taught as an artist, he was, in part, influenced by the Woodland School. In his youth, Saul was surrounded by great Native artists, including his uncle Carl Ray, a co-author and illustrator of *The Sacred Legends of the Sandy Lake Cree* (1971). The Woodland painters were known as "legend painters" for their rendering of tales and mythological characters in their work.

Educated at Red Lake High School, Saul's teachers encouraged his interests in poetry and art. As he grew up in an environment rapidly changing from the traditional to the modern, his father ensured that he was taught the stories of his people. The tales of the creation of life and nature influenced him greatly and are translated in simple images in his art. Saul feels that it is the force of nature that guides his hand to paint and many of his paintings show the simple correlation between man, animal, nature, and the spirit world.

Saul's paintings have been on exhibit in Edmonton, Saskatoon, Winnipeg, Toronto, and Ottawa. Prints of his works are distributed by the Great Canadian Print Company of Winnipeg.

Saul now lives and paints in Thunder Bay. He has four daughters, Melanie, Miriam, Lana, and Jessica, and one son, Jonah Saul. He and his wife Barbara are graduates of the Bible School at Desoronto.

ILLUSTRATIONS

Title	Page
"Sat the dreaming Wabanooqua"	12
"Once again she dwelt in childhood"	15
"When he came in shadow-silence"	16
"Came the neighbors to the wigwam"	19
"Natowè, the Snake, the cruel"	20
"Gravely rose and faced the sachems"	24
"Then they lay about the lodge-fire"	27
"How it rested on the Turtle"	28
"Till each brother's hand was lifted"	31
"Came the great horned beast, Choojaska"	32
"Mank the Loon, exhausted, lifeless"	38

"Sat the dreaming Wabanooqua"

By a curve of singing river
In the land of Mississaugas,
Sat the dreaming Wabanooqua,
Maiden Daughter-of-the-Morning.
And the maiden's eyes were tender,
Brown and limpid as the shadows
Where the musing river loiters
Underneath the drooping willows.

Now the level rays of evening
Smote across the winding valley,
Burnishing her hair with lustre
Like the plumage of a blackbird.
Overhead the tumbling swallows
Twittered in ecstatic spirals
Through the golden sea that flooded
All the silhouetted pine-trees.

Ancient elms that sprayed the sunset
With their fountain-showers of greeness,
Thrust out slowly lengthening shadows
To the eastward, yet she saw not:
Saw not anything, nor heeded.
Still she dreamed with chin uptilted,
Ember eyes of dream-lit brooding,
Eyes that mirrored back the sunset,
Mirrored flame-sheathed pines, but saw not.

Once again she dwelt in childhood,
Saw the Mississauga village,
Heard the restless village children,
Dreamed her truant feet still stumbled
On the forest paths that called her:
Saw the gentle Manoonooding,
Pleasant-Wind, whose womb had borne her,
Turn aside with tireless patience
To pursue those fleeing footsteps:
Heard once more the mild inflections
Fall from mother-lips that chided.
So a breeze that stirs the forest,
Whispers through a fragrant balsam.

"Once again she dwelt in childhood"

"When he came in shadow-silence"

Once again she saw the Chieftain
Sky-that-Slopes, that silent warrior:
He whose fatherhood had chilled her,
Stayed her childish feet from dancing.
Fell a hush across her chatter
When he came in shadow-silence
Loping through the woodland stillness;
Casting them laconic greeting,
Guttural-tongued and full of grimness.
So he came to them at evening,
From the forest's heart at sundown,
Came and squatted by the wigwam.

Once again on Autumn evenings
When the frost had kissed the meadows,
Came the neighbors to the wigwam,
Crouched about the fire and gossiped.
Wabanooqua sat and listened.

From her perch beside the ridge-pole
Where the sleeping children huddled,
Sleeping all but Wabanooqua.
Up among the skins and weapons
Where the yellow corn-stalks dangled
Till the ears were fit for shelling,
Here she sat with eyes of wonder,
Peering downward through the wood-smoke:
Saw the ruddy flame-tongues flicker
Lighting up the smoky concave;
Heard the crack of sputtering pine-knots.
Saw the restless play of firelight
On the ring of dusky faces:
Flaring gleams of tawny crimson
Dancing fitful shadow dances
On the walls of wrinkled spruce-bark.

Out beyond the blackened opening
Where the pungent wood-smoke filtered,
Frosty constellations twinkled
Through the weaving boughs of hemlock.

"Came the neighbors to the wigwam"

"Natowè, the Snake, the cruel"

There she heard how Mississauga
Yielded tribute to the stranger;
Natowè, the Snake, the cruel,
From the land of Nundawaono.
How the foe had come like blackflies
Wasting all the land before them:
Bringing fire and death and torture,
Leaving ashes and defilement.

In the moon of maple budding
When the wild-geese flying northward
Called the frozen earth to waken,
Came each year the painted rabble
Creeping through the tangled thicket,
Natowè, the Snake, the cruel,
Bearing death and desolation,
Till the very forest trembled
When the dreaded name was whispered:
Till the people's spirit fainted;
Curdled was the blood within them
When the war-whoop split the stillness.

Once again she seemed to listen,
Saw the play of flame and shadow,
Heard the rumbling drone of voices,
Heard again her people's story.

How the stricken land had suffered
Scourge of war and plague of famine
Till the villages were empty,
Waste and desolate the cornlands.

Heard how after many summers
Natowè, the Snake, had summoned
Mississauga chiefs in council,
Offered them ignoble respite.

"You shall dwell in peace," they proffered,
"You shall be as our own people:
Only give us food and weapons.
Be our bond-men. Pay us tribute!"

"Give us arrow-heads and axes,
Bring us poison for our arrows,
Give us bark and belts of wampum,
Make us coats of moose and deerskin.

"Bring us casks of fish and bear's grease,
Give us ochre and vermilion,
Bring us beans and yellow pumpkins,
Grow us corn and dig us copper.

"So with lucent oil of sunflowers
And the leaves of sweet tobacco
You shall fill our souls with plenty,
You shall rest in our protection.
Let this warfare cease between us.
Give us pledge, and smoke the peace-pipe."

So with honeyed words and crafty
Spake the Natowè in council,
And the people's soul was troubled
For their hearts were turned to water.

"Gravely rose and faced the sachems"

In the lodge a silence hovered.
Then a Mississauga stripling
Flung his deerskin round him boldly,
Gravely rose and faced the sachems.
"Are ye mad, O Mississaugas?
Are ye blinded with your terror,
That ye sell your souls for safety,
Barter with a nation's honor?
As the starving deer is fattened,
Fed and watered for the killing,
So the Natowè beguiles us,
Seeks to save our scattered remnant.
Shall the she-wolf change in fawning?
Will ye seek a Snake's protection?"

Then the Natowè were angered,
Rocked upon their yellow haunches,
Drew their knees above their foreheads,
Muttered in their greasy deerskins.
Stern uprose a grizzled war-chief,
Said--"These people are but madmen.
Let them perish in their folly.
Let the forest close upon them!"

Then the Mississauga women
Listening through the walls of spruce-bark,
Bent their foreheads in the leaf-mould,
Beat upon their breasts with weeping.
Thus the milder counsels triumphed,
Thus the peoples smoked the peace-pipe.

Thus she heard her people's story,
Heard the tales they told in winter
When the snows were deep and drifting,
When the bitter north-wind whistled.

Then they lay about the lodge-fire,
Munched the Wabimin, the apple,
Roasted cakes upon the embers:
Propped their chins up with their elbows,
Listened to the story-tellers.

"Never tell a tale in summer
Lest the animals should hear you:
Lest they hear and be offended:
In your bed the toads come creeping.
Winter is the time for stories.
Never tell your tales in summer!"

"Then they lay about the lodge-fire"

"How it rested on the Turtle"

Thus she heard the old traditions,
Heard the legends of her people
Handed down the misty ages
Through succeeding generations.

Thus she heard the ancient stories,
Heard the tales of awe and wonder:
How the world was first created:
How it rested on the Turtle.

How the Little Turtle clambered
Up the sky and gathered thunder:
Made the lights, the Wasakwoni:
Made the sun to rule the daytime:
Made the moon and stars for darkness.

Thus she heard of Nanabozho
In the long-ago beginning,
In the days before the deluge
When the sons of men were stalwart.
How the oki rested on him:
How his goodness made him mighty.

But the sons of men were evil,
Grew more wicked as they prospered,
Till each brother's hand was lifted
Up in wrath against his brother,
And the earth was filled with anger.

Then the great primeval monsters
Swayed with fury like their masters,
Rent the air with mighty snortings,
Charged and met in deadly combat:
Till the earth was full of slaughter
And the rivers flowed with blood.

"Till each brother's hand was lifted"

"Came the great horned beast, Choojaska"

From his lair ascending slowly
Came the great horned beast, Choojaska:
Stood upon a hill and bellowed:
Stood and bid the world defiance.

In a cave beneath the mountains
Omukiki heard and heeded,
He, the Toad, the Water-Keeper,
From whose belly all the rivers
Issued forth to slake the land.

He the Keeper of the Waters,
Heard the challenge from the hill-top,
Heard the great horned beast who bellowed:
Shook with wrath until the waters
Clashed like thunder in his belly.

Then the earth was rocked with combat:
Thunders, lightnings split the heavens:
Forests splintered in the whirlwind:
Fire and earthquake rent the mountains.

From the caverns of his belly
Omukiki belched a torrent,
Swirled a flood at every footstep,
Battered back the great Choojaska,
Smothered him with angry waters;
Till a rush of tumbling fury
Flung the beast upon a rock cliff.

Whence he paused a moment, breathless,
Like a thunderbolt descended,
Smote the great toad from above him,
Thrust his great horn through his belly:
Brought upon the world the deluge.

So the waters slowly mounted
Till they covered every valley:
Slowly covered up the lowlands:
Gently lapped about the foothills:
Thrust long fingers up the mountains,

So the waters wrought destruction,
Covered up the mightiest cedars.
In the villages and forests
Every living creature perished.

Nanabozho, in a vision
Warned of what should come upon them,
Fled toward the land of sundown,
Sought him out the highest mountain.

At the summit paused in kindness,
Saw the animals stampeding,
Stooped and chose him male and female,
One of each thrust in his bosom.

Twain of beasts of field and forest,
Twain of creeping things and wild-fowl,
Twain of singing birds he chose him,
Held them in his breast securely:
Saw the hungry waters rising,
Chose in haste the loftiest cedar,
Leaped to safety in its branches.

Nanabozho still ascending
Step by step beyond the waters,
Plucked the branches as he passed them,
Thrust the green boughs in his girdle.

When he reached the very tree-top
Nanabozho stood and chanted,
Sang and beat upon his long-bow,
Beat the rhythm with an arrow.

As he chanted grew the cedar,
Grew a span with every measure;
Just beyond the swirling waters
Lifted up its topmost branches.

When at last the song grew weary
Nanabozho loosed his girdle,
Formed a raft of boughs of cedar,
Ventured on the waste of waters:
Saw no mountain peak nor tree-top,
Saw no spruce against the sky-line,
Saw no life, but water only,
Water an the left and right hand,
Water to the last horizon.

Forty days the sun ascended
Out of endless waters eastward,
Sank in endless waters westward:
Still the raft of cedar drifted.

When the full days were accomplished
Nanabozho said: "My children,
Let us make another dry land:
Let us make a place to dwell in.
Mank the Loon, the mighty diver,
He shall bring us earth for building:
Grains of sand to make an island:
Form a new world from the old one."

Then across the lonely waters
Rang the diver's plaintive quaver;
Thrice repeated: mystic: eerie:
Full of mournfulness and yearning.
Thus the loon departed from them:
Sang, and sank without a ripple,

"Mank the Loon, exhausted, lifeless"

On the morning of the third day
Nanabozho peering over,
Saw a huddled bunch of feathers
Rising from the depths beneath him:
Mank the Loon, exhausted, lifeless;
Bringing back no earth for building.

Tenderly did Nanabozho
Take the diver in his bosom,
Breathed the breath of life upon him;
Said: "Awake my gallant birdling!"
Till the languid heartbeats fluttered
With the thrill of life returning.

Nanabozho said: "My children,
Let us honor Mank the Diver!
Though the work seem unavailing,
He shall save his life who gives it.
Who shall follow his example?
Who will mock at death as he did?"

Cried the skillful swimmers saying,
"Let us go, O Nanabozho!
Let us dare the sunless fathoms,
Seek the precious earth for building."
Till he smiled upon them saying:
"He that gives his life shall find it."

Thus the otter, webfoot Nigik,
Perished in the green abysses:
Likewise Ahmik, he the beaver,
Paddle-tail the cunning Builder:
But the Master breathed upon them,
With compassion he restored them:
Gave them life again and breathing.

When thrice forty days were ended
Spoke the humble muskrat saying,
"I have waited, gracious Master,
Lest my words should seem presumption:
Lest a fool be found to venture
Where the mighty find defeat.

"Yet the depths are still unconquered:
Still we ride the waste of waters,
For the swimmers are exhausted,
And the mightiest have failed.

"Send me, therefore, o my Master,
Lest this company should perish.
Though this lot be poor and lowly,
Let the humble Wajak go!"

Nanabozho smiled and answered,
"He is great who serves his fellows.
Let the Wajak try his fortune:
Let him bring us earth to build with."

On the morning of the third day
Nanabozho looked before him,
Saw a ripple in the water,
Saw the weary Wajak swimming.

Tenderly he leaned and took him
In his arms, all spent and gasping;
Nestled him within his bosom;
Chanted proudly to the sunrise.

"O thou shining sun, Segosku,
Mightiest father of the daylight,
Smile upon this little Wajak;
Clothe him with a shining sunbeam.
Let the Wajak be exalted:
He hath brought us earth for building!"

'By thy brightness, O Segosku;
By thy shining face I swear it,
While the world I build endureth,
Wajak's race shall never perish.

"Each succeeding year increasing
They shall be as stars in number.
Honor to the lowly Wajak:
In humility is greatness!

"Lend thine aid, thou great Segosku:
Sparkle on these precious earth-grains.
Soon thy face shall see an island:
Soon a cedar tree shall greet thee.
Thou shalt kiss a rustling forest:
Linger in the pleasant valleys.

"Soon no more shall endless waters
Mirror back thy face at dawning:
From the void dry land arises.
Nanabozho builds a new world!"

Thus he took him seven earth grains,
Crushed them in his hands to powder,
Cast it on the boughs of cedar;
Blew upon it softly, saying:
"Hear my voice O earth--Awaken!"

Thus a new world came to being,
Rested on the raft of cedar:
Spread itself in rolling meadows:
Shouldered up the pine-clad mountains.

When it grew beyond his vision
Nanabozho called the Mainggen,
Sent the wolf to run across it,
Measured by the time it took him.

First the journey took but one day:
Then he blew again and sent him,
Till it took the Mainggen five days:
Five days: ten days: then a full moon:
After that a year: then five years:
Till at last when Nanabozho
Sent a young wolf on the journey
It was old before the finish;
Died before the journey's ending.

Thus the new world was completed.
Nanabozho said: "'Tis ended!"
Journeyed through his new creation,
Made the different tribes upon it:
Gave them languages and customs:
Taught the red man his religion:
Led him in the ways of knowledge.

Still within the frozen arctic
When the northern lights are flaring,
Nanabozho sits and watches,
Sends up signals to his people.

G L O S S A R Y

The words with asterisks (*) are ones which appear in Chamberlain's researches.

*Ahmik,	the Beaver. Chamberlain gives amik as the spelling.
Choojaska,	the Great Horned Beast. Chamberlain says that choojas was the Mississauga word for ugly nose.
*Mainggen,	the Wolf. Also given in Chamberlain as myeengun.
*Mank,	the Loon. Wabimank (or the white loon) is given by Chamberlain as a mythological figure.
*Manoonooding,	or Pleasant-Wind, the Mother of Wabanooqua. Chamberlain lists this name as one of the chiefs of the Credit Reserve.
*Nanabozho,	the Great Spirit
*Natowè,	the Snake. The Mississauga word for the Iroquois.
*Nigik,	the Otter
Nundawaono,	the Land of the Snake People
Oki,	heart or spirit
*Omukiki,	the Toad, the Water-Keeper. Variously given in Chamberlain as the toad; the frog; "the hairless", the name of a mythological character (who helps the rabbit to kill the moose).
Sachems,	supreme chiefs
*Segosku,	the Rising Sun. Also given as Segoskee in Chamberlain.
*Sky-that-Slopes,	the Chieftain, Father of Wabanooqua. Chamberlain lists Nahwahjekezhegwaby (meaning "sky that slopes") as chief of the Credit Reserve in 1830.
Wabanooqua,	Maiden Daughter-of-the-Morning
*Wabimin,	the Apple. Wabimin means "white fruit" according to Chamberlain.
*Wajak,	the Muskrat. Spelled wajask or wadjack in Chamberlain, a mythological character who figures in the Deluge legend.
*Wasakwoni,	the Northern Lights. Chamberlain lists this word as the Mississauga word for light.

REFERENCES

CHAMBERLAIN, ALEXANDER FRANCIS. 1888. "Notes on the History, Customs, and Beliefs of the Mississagua Indians," *Journal of American Folk-lore,* 1: 150-160; and other articles on the Mississaugas: 2: 141-147 (1889), 3: 149-154 (1890), 4: 193-213 (1891)

CHAMBERLAIN, ALEXANDER FRANCIS. 1888. *Notes on the History, Customs, and Beliefs of the Mississaguas,* Cambridge: Riverside Press

CHAMBERLAIN, ALEXANDER FRANCIS. 1892. *The Language of the Mississaga Indians of Skugog: A Contribution to the Linguistics of the Algonkian Tribes of Canada.* Philadelphia: MacCalla

JONES, PETER. 1861. *History of the Ojebway Indians: With Especial Reference to Their Conversion to Christianity.* London: A.W. Bennett; reprinted 1970: Freeport, N.Y.: Books for Librairies

SMITH, DONALD B. 1975. "Who Are the Mississauga?" *Ontario History,* 67: 211-222

SMITH DONALD B. 1987. *Sacred Feathers: The Reverend Peter Jones (Kahkewaquonaby) and the Mississauga Indians.* Toronto: University of Toronto Press

TRIGGER, BRUCE G., ed. 1978. *Handbook of North American Indians:* Vol. 15: *The Northeast.* Washington, D.C.: Smithsonian Institute